CHITCHAT

Celebrating the World's Languages

WRITTEN BY **JUDE ISABELLA**

ILLUSTRATED BY **KATHY BOAKE**

Kids Can Press

Do m'Aint Pat, ag gluaiseacht chun cinn i gcónaí,
ag treabhadh an ghoirt do chách — J.I.

To my family with love: my husband Bruno,
which means brown; my son Beau, meaning handsome;
and my daughter Belle, beautiful — K.B.

Acknowledgments

A big thank you to the academics, friends and friends of friends who lent their native tongues, expertise and enthusiasm to this project. Any errors are my own. Special thanks to Henry Davis (Dept. of Linguistics, University of British Columbia) for taking the time to read over the manuscript. And thanks to: Hashem Ahmadzadeh (College of Social Sciences and International Studies, University of Exeter), Veronika Ambros (Slavic Dept., University of Toronto), Douglas Bigham (Dept. of Linguistics & Asian/Middle Eastern Languages, San Diego State University), Laurel Bowman (Greek and Roman Studies, University of Victoria), Ewa Czaykowska-Higgins (Dept. of Linguistics, University of Victoria), Máirín Nic Dhiarmada (Celtic Studies, University of Toronto), John Dyson (Emeritus, Dept. of Linguistics, Indiana University), Virginia Evans (English instructor, University of British Columbia), Jila Ghomeshi (Dept. of Linguistics, University of Manitoba), K. David Harrison (Dept. of Linguistics, Swarthmore College), John Hewson (Dept. of Linguistics, Memorial University), Iain Higgins (Dept. of English, University of Victoria), Hua Lin (Dept. of Linguistics, University of Victoria), Dianne Newbury (Wellcome Trust Centre for Human Genetics, University of Oxford), April Nowell (Dept. of Anthropology, University of Victoria), Tom Palaima (Director, Program in Aegean Scripts and Prehistory, University of Texas, Austin), Drew Rendall (Dept. of Psychology, University of Lethbridge), John Ross (Cherokee Nation Translation Department), Nigel Strudwick (Dept. of Art History, University of Memphis), Doug Trick (School of Graduate Studies, Linguistics, Trinity Western University), Hiroto Uchihara (Dept. of Linguistics, University of Buffalo), Sakoieta' Widrick (Indigenous Studies, Brock University) and Erin Wilkinson (Dept. of Linguistics, University of Manitoba). Also thanks to bilingual and multilingual people (musicians, accountants, writers, lawyers, biologists, farmers) who are many times over human beings: Arthur Arnold (Dutch), Eva Bild (French), David Butvill (Spanish), Rhitu Chatterjee (Bengali), Rhona Ní Chearbhaill (Gaelic), Molly Chythlook (Yup'ik), Ross Crockford (Czech), Martin Gelzinis (Lithuanian), Mina Isota (Japanese), Laima Ivule and friends (Latvian/Lithuanian), Yeongha Jung (Korean), Nomi Kaston (Hebrew), Karen LaViolette-Nibe (Japanese), Margaret Mason (Legalese/French), Julia Naimska (Polish), Tomás Ó h-Íde (Gaelic), Kim Stokes and friends (Dutch/Russian), Andrew Whitson (Swedish) and Woktela (Yuchi).

Text © 2013 Jude Isabella
Illustrations © 2013 Kathy Boake

Blissymbolics symbols, page 35: © Blissymbolics Communication International: www.blissymbolics.org. Reproduced with permission of Blissymbolics Communication International.

Kids Can Press acknowledges the financial support of the Government of Ontario, through the Ontario Media Development Corporation's Ontario Book Initiative; the Ontario Arts Council; the Canada Council for the Arts; and the Government of Canada, through the CBF, for our publishing activity.

Published in Canada by
Kids Can Press Ltd.
25 Dockside Drive
Toronto, ON M5A 0B5

www.kidscanpress.com

Published in the U.S. by
Kids Can Press Ltd.
2250 Military Road
Tonawanda, NY 14150

The artwork in this book was rendered in Photoshop.
The text is set in Cantoria.

Edited by Valerie Wyatt
Designed by Julia Naimska

This book is smyth sewn casebound.
Manufactured in Shenzhen, China, in 3/2013 by C & C Offset

CM 13 0 9 8 7 6 5 4 3 2 1

Library and Archives Canada Cataloguing in Publication

Isabella, Jude
    Chitchat : celebrating the world's languages / written by Jude Isabella ; illustrated by Kathy Boake.

Includes index.
ISBN 978-1-55453-787-7

    1. Language and languages — Juvenile literature.
I. Boake, Kathy II. Title.

P107.I73 2013   j401   C2012-908049-7

Kids Can Press is a **Corus**™ Entertainment company

CONTENTS

LET'S CHITCHAT

The key to being a talker? It's all in your head. See Page 11.

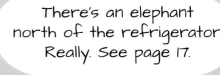

There's an elephant north of the refrigerator. Really. See page 17.

When you began to talk, you learned at least 10 new words a day. For more about your baby talk, see page 6.

SPEAK UP!

WHEN YOU WERE BORN, you probably wailed your head off — it's a real shocker, the real world. Your "wah, wah" said something like: "It's freezing out here!" or "Can someone turn off that stupid light?" Everyone in the room got your point, even though you hadn't used any words.

Crying and throwing things work for a while, but soon get frustrating because people are liable to misunderstand you. ("No, my diaper isn't wet. I want food!") To get what you really want, you need language. ("Ba-na-na!")

By age two, you had mastered about 200 words. You picked them up by listening to the people around you, especially your parents. "Mama" and "Dada" had to be careful what they said — you were learning 10 or more new words a day, sometimes one new word every 90 minutes. All this while still wearing a diaper.

At age three, even though you couldn't tie your shoes or make yourself a sandwich, you were a sophisticated talker. Having language allowed you to communicate that you needed help with dressing and eating and many other things. By age four, you could say complicated things like: "I want shoes with Velcro like the ones in that shoe store we went to. Remember? Before we ate lunch." About this time, you probably also started to read simple words and draw letters. And now, you speak, read and write so well that you can read this book.

It's through language that babies and children acquire knowledge and values and the other things that make us human. As far as we know, no other animal can communicate the way humans do. Only we can combine sounds into words and arrange words into an infinite number of sentences to talk about the past, present and future. Some gorillas and chimps can learn sign language and use and understand simple sentences, but "if-then" statements stump them. For example, "If you say please, then I'll give you a banana." And no gorilla or chimp could decode something as complicated as this: "Katie wishes Juan hadn't stopped Hector from giving a banana to the chimp, since the chimp said please." Got it?

> BY THE TIME YOU'RE FINISHED HIGH SCHOOL, YOU'LL HAVE A VOCABULARY OF ABOUT 20 000 WORDS.

Gaa goo!

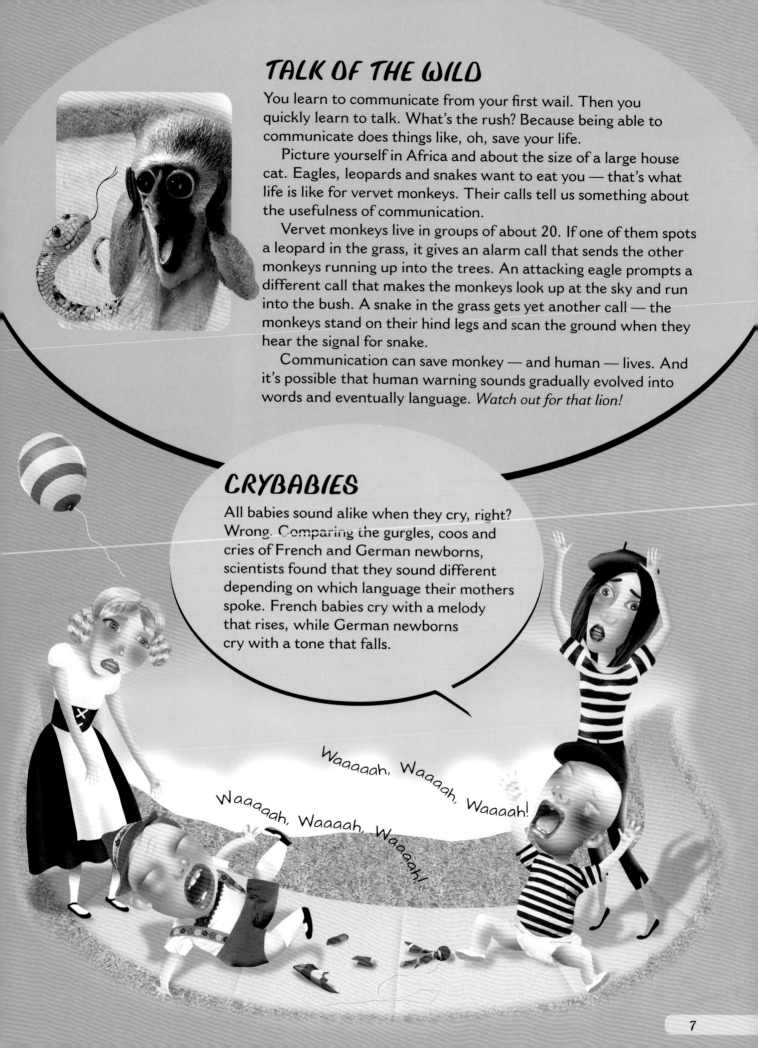

TALK OF THE WILD

You learn to communicate from your first wail. Then you quickly learn to talk. What's the rush? Because being able to communicate does things like, oh, save your life.

Picture yourself in Africa and about the size of a large house cat. Eagles, leopards and snakes want to eat you — that's what life is like for vervet monkeys. Their calls tell us something about the usefulness of communication.

Vervet monkeys live in groups of about 20. If one of them spots a leopard in the grass, it gives an alarm call that sends the other monkeys running up into the trees. An attacking eagle prompts a different call that makes the monkeys look up at the sky and run into the bush. A snake in the grass gets yet another call — the monkeys stand on their hind legs and scan the ground when they hear the signal for snake.

Communication can save monkey — and human — lives. And it's possible that human warning sounds gradually evolved into words and eventually language. *Watch out for that lion!*

CRYBABIES

All babies sound alike when they cry, right? Wrong. Comparing the gurgles, coos and cries of French and German newborns, scientists found that they sound different depending on which language their mothers spoke. French babies cry with a melody that rises, while German newborns cry with a tone that falls.

Waaaaah, Waaaah, Waaaah!

Waaaaah, Waaaah, Waaaah!

LANGUAGE IS ...

GRAMMAR DAY IS MARCH 4!

BOOK YOU WAY RULES of any is without there understand no this would.

What?! A fully developed language has rules for combining words into sentences. These rules are called grammar. Apply the rules of English grammar to the sentence above and you get this: "Without rules there is no way you would understand any of this book."

Every language also has syntax, and syntax rules vary from language to language. Take something as simple as word order. In English, you would never say: "My homework an elephant ate!" Nor would you say: "Ate my homework an elephant!"

English uses a Subject-Verb-Object (SVO) word order most of the time.

An elephant	ate	my homework.
[Subject]	[Verb]	[Object]

Other languages with an SVO word order, such as Italian, use different word orders some of the time. Many Asian languages — Korean, for example — use a Subject-Object-Verb (SOV) word order.

코끼리가	내 숙제를	먹었다.
Ko-ggi-ri-ga	*nae suk-jae-reul*	*mok-ot-da.*
[Subject]	[Object]	[Verb]

An elephant	my homework	ate.
[Subject]	[Object]	[Verb]

Irish Gaelic uses a Verb-Subject-Object (VSO) word order.

D'ith	*eilifint*	*m'obair bhaile.*
[Verb]	[Subject]	[Object]

Ate	an elephant	my homework.
[Verb]	[Subject]	[Object]

SVO and SOV are the most common word orders, followed by VSO and VOS. OVS and OSV are rare word orders. And just to make things more complicated, some languages have no main word order. Kanyen'kéha speakers of the Mohawk First Nation use words and word order to change the meaning of a sentence. For example:

Kenòn:we's.	*I like it.*
Kenòn:we's ní:'i.	I *like* it.
Í:'i kenòn:we's.	*I* like it.

Interestingly, we don't always think in the same word order that we speak. For example, when giving instructions nonverbally (without speaking), people — regardless of their language — use the SOV word order.

How to …

Teach four friends how to do something, such as how to find a book at the library. Use spoken language with two of the friends and silent body gestures with the other two. Which method is more efficient?

CRASH BLOSSOMS

Writing newspaper headlines is hard. A headline has to be short and punchy, lure in readers and make sense. Sometimes the result is what's called a "crash blossom." The term was coined in 2009 after the newspaper *Japan Today* ran a headline that read: "Violinist Linked to JAL Crash Blossoms." (The article was about a violinist whose career was blossoming, and whose father had died in a JAL plane crash.)

Try guessing the real meanings behind these ones:
- "Leftover Turkey Hunting Licenses Available" (Associated Press, August 20, 2010)
- "Debate Continues on Cell Phones While Driving" (*Burlington Free Press*, April 30, 2010)
- "Baby Steps to New Life-Forms" (*New York Times*, May 27, 2010)
- "Cop Shows Highlight of New Fall TV Season" (National Public Radio website, September 16, 2010)
- "Man Shot in Chest, Leg Knocks on Door for Help" (*Dayton Daily News*, February 12, 2010)

HERE LIES THE BODY OF JONATHAN GROUND, WHO WAS LOST AT SEA AND NEVER FOUND.

HOW LANGUAGE CAME TO BE

LANGUAGE LEAVES BEHIND no bones or artifacts, so figuring out when humans first began using it is tough. Over the years, linguists (people who study languages) have come up with some interesting theories.

In the late 1800s, a self-taught French linguist named Jean-Pierre Brisset theorized that early humans mimicked frogs and this evolved into language — the French language, that is. The frog sound "koa koa" became *quoi? quoi?* ("what? what?"). And the frog sound "brekekekex" became *qu'est-ce que c'est?* ("what is it?"). The "ribbiting" truth? No. Better guesses about how language came to be involve music.

Cuddle a newborn baby and you may find yourself cooing and talking in a singsongy way. Music is found in all cultures, which suggests that it might be hardwired into our brains. Some other species also have music. Monkeys, for example, recognize clashing musical tones, and songbirds sing in tune and have rhythm. It's possible that in humans, early musical sounds morphed into speaking sounds. But why did language evolve only in humans? Why not talking monkeys, chimps or apes? Partly because we have the right vocal equipment.

As a baby, you could breathe through your nose as you ate because your larynx was higher in your throat than it is now — just like in an ape. (The larynx is an organ in the neck that allows you to produce sounds and stops you from inhaling food.) This high-placed larynx prevented baby-you (and apes) from making some sounds that you now can easily make. As you grew, your larynx dropped lower and your chances of choking while eating rose, but so did your ability to make new sounds. Not so for apes.

Human tongues are also more flexible and mobile than the tongues of apes and monkeys. Our tongues move around our teeth, lips and the roofs of our mouths when we talk, allowing us a huge range of sounds.

Just think, slight changes in our anatomy made us the chatterboxes of the animal world.

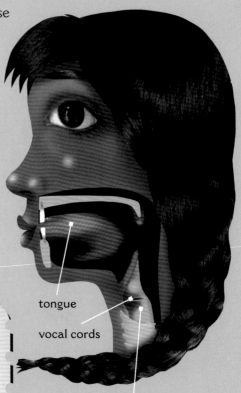

tongue

vocal cords

larynx

Sound Symbols

Some scientists think that the first words might have reflected the sound of an object or action and that these "sound words" may have been a stepping-stone to language. Other linguists think the sound connection is random.

Do words in some way "match" objects or actions? Try this word/sound test used by linguists. They asked non-Japanese speakers to match the Japanese word to an English word. See how you score, then test other people. (Answers on page 43.) A consistent score of six or higher suggests that there may be a connection between a word and a sound.

1. *akarui*
   a) bright or b) dark

2. *amai*
   a) sweet or b) sour

3. *nameraka*
   a) rough or b) smooth

4. *aruku*
   a) walk or b) run

5. *hayai*
   a) slow or b) fast

6. *hitotsu*
   a) many or b) one

7. *katai*
   a) hard or b) soft

8. *yaseta*
   a) fat or b) thin

9. *mijikai*
   a) short or b) long

10. *nageru*
    a) throw or b) catch

WHEN A WORD SOUNDS LIKE THE OBJECT OR ACTION IT DESCRIBES, IT'S CALLED "ONOMATOPOEIA" (AH-NO-MAH-TA-PEEA). SOME EXAMPLES ARE "SNIFF," "HICCUP" AND "BANG." CAN YOU THINK OF OTHERS?

TALKING IN (GENETIC) CODE

SWAP A BABY FROM England with a baby from Tanzania, and the two babies will grow up speaking the language that is spoken to them. However, swap the English baby with a chimpanzee from Tanzania, and not only will you be in a lot of trouble, but the chimpanzee will never speak either language. As far as we know, only humans can learn to speak.

Some linguists think language might be hardwired into our genes. Genes are the part of DNA that passes on hereditary information from parents to offspring. For example, genes passed from your parents to you determined your hair and eye colors. Scientists think we also have genes that control speech and language, such as a gene called *FOXP2*.

FOXP2 is like a motherboard for speech. A motherboard allows the different parts of your computer to talk to one another. No motherboard, no communication. In humans, *FOXP2* is probably one of many "motherboard" genes. They tell the other genes involved with speech and language what to do.

People with a broken version of the *FOXP2* gene can talk, but they have little control over their lips, tongues and mouths, which makes them difficult to understand. Scientists know this because of a family in Britain. Out of 37 family members, from great-grandparents to great-grandkids, 15 have trouble speaking. Of the 15, some have problems with grammar and written language as well. All also have identical *FOXP2* genes that are different from the normal version of the gene.

So *FOXP2* is the language gene, right? Nope. Your pet cat, dog, hamster or mouse has a *FOXP2* gene, too. In fact, most animals going back to the time of the dinosaurs have some version of it, though slightly different from the human version. Only songbirds that learn songs throughout their lives have a *FOXP2* gene that is almost identical to the human version of the gene.

The slight changes to the human form of the gene probably happened about 200 000 years ago when modern humans (your ancestors) first showed up. The new form of the gene allowed humans to coordinate their facial muscles in just the right way for speech to develop, separating us from the other animals forever.

WHAT DO LIONS, TIGERS, JAGUARS AND LEOPARDS HAVE IN COMMON WITH HUMANS BUT NOT OTHER ANIMALS? A SIMILAR VOCAL TRACT. ROAR!

Er ... roar?

LANGUAGE FAMILIES

SERIO, OPUSCULUM MEUM devoravit elephas. That's Latin for: "Seriously, an elephant ate my homework."

Latin was spoken across the Roman Empire about 2000 years ago. It's no longer in use, but it was the basis for many European languages spoken today. Here's how it happened: The Romans invaded a country, settled down and sprinkled around Latin, the language they spoke. Latin mixed with the existing language and — ta-da! — a new language was born. This happened in several different places, creating different Romance (there are those Romans again!) languages. French, Spanish, Italian, Romanian and Portuguese are the major Romance languages.

The Romance languages are part of a large Indo-European language family. A language family is a group of languages that share a common ancestor language. In the Indo-European language family, there are 426 different languages, all with the same Latin ancestor.

Indo-European is just one of 116 language families around the world. The largest is the Niger-Congo family of Africa, which has 1532 languages.

In all, there are almost 7000 languages in the world's 116 language families. (All numbers are estimates. Even the experts, who have studied languages for many years, don't always agree.)

perfectus excellentia

benevolentia

bonus, melior, optimus

incredibilis

fortunatus

HERE'S A MYSTERY. ALL OF THE WORLD'S LANGUAGES GREW FROM ONE LANGUAGE, BUT NO ONE KNOWS WHAT THAT LANGUAGE WAS.

LET'S TALK ELEPHANTS

Although languages in language families are related to a common ancestor, they may or may not have much in common. For example, in English we say, "Elephants are enormous!" Here's the same sentence in some other languages in our Indo-European language family:

Latvian: *Ziloņi ir milzīgi!*
Lithuanian: *Drambliai yra milžiniški!*
Swedish: *Elefanter är enorma!*
Dutch: *Olifanten zijn enorm groot!*
Polish: *Słonie są ogromne!*

THE SKY IS ... BLACK

"BLUE SKIES, SMILING AT ME, nothing but blue skies do I see." Imagine trying to translate those song lyrics into a language that didn't have a word for blue. Until the English word "blue" was introduced to them, people on Murray Island in the South Pacific described the sky as black. "Black skies, smiling at me …"?

It turns out that what you name a color depends on the culture you come from. While most languages have words for black, white and red, not all have words for blue. Ancient Greek and Hebrew didn't, and no blues are found in ancient Indian poems. Many languages today have no word for blue, either. For example, the Tzeltal, people who live in southern Mexico, would use the word *yaš* to cover blues and greens.

Unless color-blind, humans see the same colors of the rainbow. It's how they divvy up the shades and name them that differ. Long ago, that depended on whether a color or shade was important to them. If recognizing a color helped people to survive, it got a name.

The first color usually given a name in a language is red. It's a color that excites people. Apes, including their non-hairy relatives (us), are attracted to red — it's a sign of danger (blood) and fertility. Some zoos advise visitors to avoid wearing red so the apes don't get the wrong idea.

Greens and yellows are often the next colors to be given names in a language. No surprise, considering they're the colors of vegetation and food. Recognizing (and naming) these colors helped people find food and survive. Blue, however, was less important. Very few foods are naturally blue, and naming the color of the sky or sea is not going to feed anyone.

Kids have to learn what their culture names the various colors, and they're apt to make mistakes at first. This may be because, early on, they associate colors with objects, such as a red tomato, yellow banana, gray elephant. But what color are marbles? Or sneakers?

MY DESK IS SOUTH OF THE BLACKBOARD

Like colors, direction is also cultural. In Guugu Yimithirr, an Australian aboriginal language, there are no words for "left" or "right." Nor are there words for "behind" or "in front of." Guugu Yimithirr uses the four directions of the compass: *gungaa* (north), *jiba* (south), *guwa* (west) and *naga* (east). If a hungry elephant was in your house looking for a snack, and no one noticed, you might yell out, "There's an elephant north of the refrigerator!"

Cultures in Mexico, Bali, Nepal, Namibia and Madagascar rely on directions, too.

LANGUAGE EXTINCTION

TRADE A LIFE OF FORAGING for a life of farming and you might lose more than the blisters on your feet. You might lose your mother tongue — the language you learned first.

Language extinction has been going on for thousands of years. About 10 000 years ago, when people settled down to farm, there was a big wave of language extinction. People were less isolated than they had been as foragers (hunters and gatherers of food). They lived in communities, where some groups dominated and other groups were absorbed, along with their languages.

Another language extinction wave hit when Europeans colonized the Americas and Oceania. Australia, for example, probably had 260 native languages before the British began settling the continent in 1788. Only about 100 remain.

Some linguists think that roughly 140 000 languages have been spoken at one time or another on our planet, and that 80 to 99 percent of them are extinct. Today, the rate of language extinction has sped up. Every two weeks, a language dies. By the end of this century, between half and three-quarters of the world's almost 7000 languages will vanish. The disappearing languages occur mostly in small societies that have no written tradition.

Language Lost

Of all the languages spoken today, only half are being taught to children. That means many languages are unlikely to survive into the future. Make a list of the people you know who never learned the language of their parents. Are some languages more likely to be passed on than others?

Having just a few common languages over the world is good for communication but bad for knowledge. When a language goes extinct, it takes information with it, usually about the natural world.

Take the two-barred flasher butterfly from Central America, for example. The Tzeltal people in southern Mexico have a number of names for the butterfly. To outsiders, there appear to be no differences to warrant multiple names, unless you look at the butterfly's larvae — the caterpillars. Different types of larvae eat different crops, which is important information for the Tzeltal people. So they gave each caterpillar a different name. Western scientists eventually figured out that there are, indeed, at least 10 species of the butterfly. They could have figured that out easily from the Tzeltal language.

Cultural traditions, such as important family relationships, are also lost when a language goes extinct or even changes drastically. In Old English, for example, with one word you knew if an uncle was related to your mother or your father — "eam" is the mother's brother, and "faedera" is the father's brother. When the language changed, this distinction and probably some customs were lost along with it.

When a community with one language is surrounded by a more dominant language, the less dominant language often loses out. For example, in Bolivia about 60 percent of the population are Native peoples who speak several different Native languages. Spanish speakers surround them, and Spanish is the second most spoken mother tongue in the world (the first is Chinese). The Native languages have been overwhelmed by Spanish, which is a useful language to know when dealing with the outside world.

MATUWUHOU! *THAT'S WHAT A SPEAKER OF TORATAN WOULD SAY IF HE WOKE UP ONE MORNING AND FOUND SOMETHING HAD CHANGED — FOR INSTANCE, IF HE HAD FALLEN OUT OF BED.*

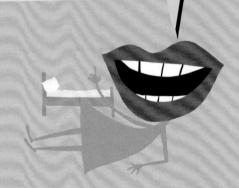

LANGUAGE BY NUMBERS

- 4 percent of the world's languages have gone extinct since 1950
- 43 percent of the world's languages are endangered
- 80 percent of the world's population communicates in 83 languages
- 90 percent of languages do not exist on the Internet

LANGUAGES IN DANGER

LET'S SAY YOU LIVE in East Jabib and you speak Watooshee (neither exists), and you're surrounded by people who speak Nebisky (it's made up, too). Nebisky is the language used in the market because it's a common language that everyone can speak and understand. Nebisky is also a written language, a handy thing in the market when you need to keep records.

Now imagine you're older and have children. To make sure your kids will do well in life, you want to make sure they know Nebisky. Other parents do the same with their children — everyone wants their kids to succeed. Before you know it, Watooshee is barely used except by old people. In a generation or two, Watooshee becomes an endangered language, at risk of dying out.

This is one way languages become extinct. It has happened — and continues to happen — around the world. Languages can also be lost when one group dominates the government and outlaws the language of another group. When Turkey became a republic in 1923, it banned the Kurdish language. Kurdish people make up about 20 percent of Turkey's population. In 1991, Kurds were allowed to speak their language, but it still could not be taught in public schools.

Sometimes outlawing a language is more subtle. In Canada, the United States, Australia and New Zealand, for example, Native children who had their own languages were sent away from home to attend schools in English. The schools eventually closed, but by then many Native languages lost an entire generation of speakers.

Linguists have identified several hot spots where languages are in the most danger.

Siberia: 16 language families are in danger. Tofa has only about 25 speakers. When they're gone, Tofa speakers will take with them a unique suffix. (A suffix is something attached to the end of a word — for example, "s" at the end of "dog" makes it plural.) The suffix *sig* in Tofa means "to smell like." Tack *sig* onto the end of *ivi* and you get *ivisig*, which means someone smells like ... a reindeer.

North America: 28 language families are endangered. A man named Bud Lane is the only fluent speaker of Siletz Dee-ni. And Siletz Dee-ni is the last of the 27 languages once spoken on the Siletz reservation in Oregon. In the southwest, only a handful of people speak Yuchi. It's a unique language — it's not related to any other language.

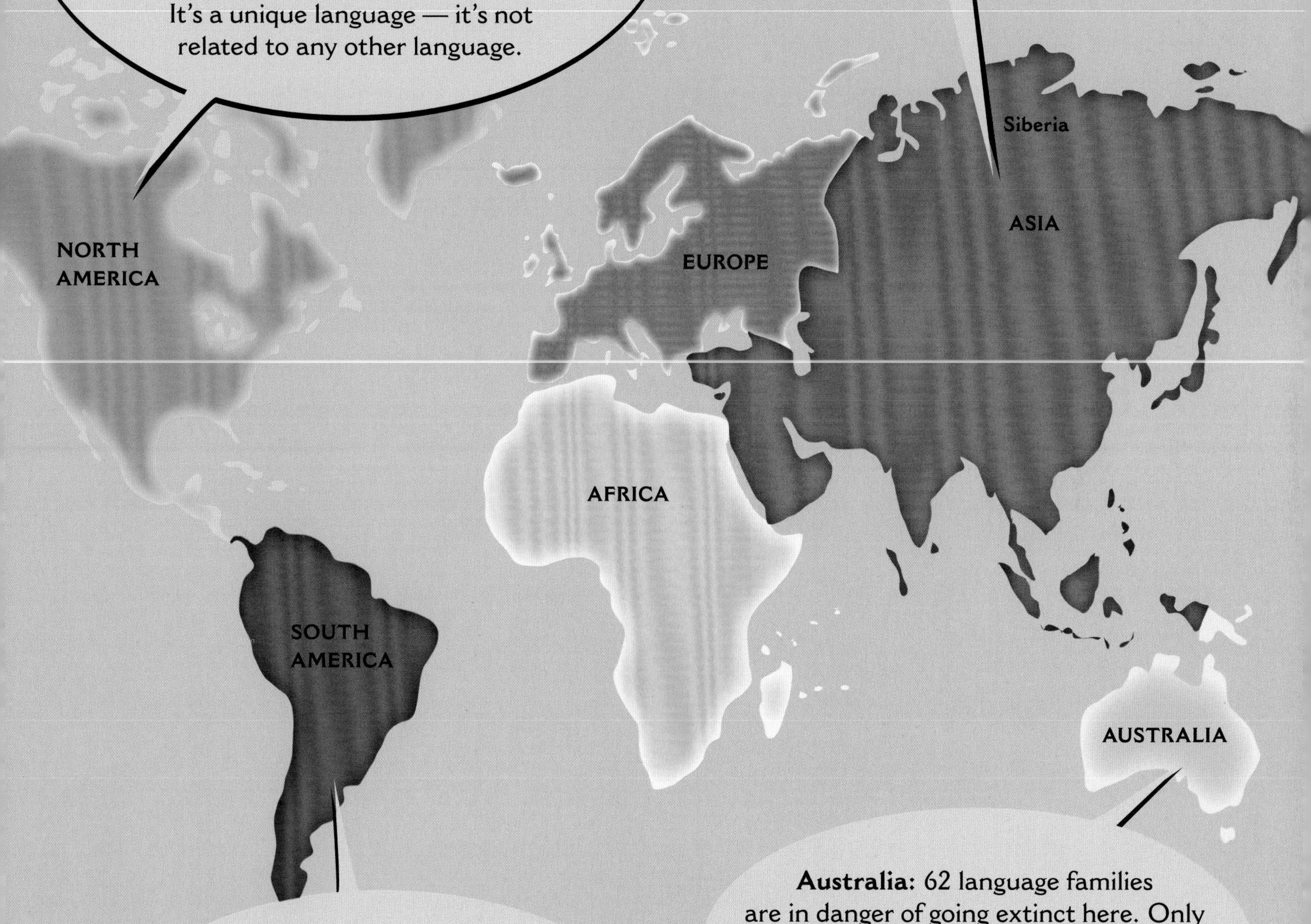

Siberia

ASIA

EUROPE

NORTH
AMERICA

AFRICA

SOUTH
AMERICA

AUSTRALIA

South America: 94 language families are in danger of becoming extinct, including the Bolivian language Kallawaya. It's a second (and secret) language spoken only by men and passed from father to son, or grandfather to grandson.

Australia: 62 language families are in danger of going extinct here. Only three people speak Magati Ke fluently, three speak Yawuru, and only one man, Charlie Mangulda, speaks Amurdag.

SAVING LANGUAGES

PRAWO JAZDY. The name was infamous in Ireland — Jazdy had racked up speeding tickets and parking fines all over the country. He had at least 50 violations and yet he had never been convicted.

An enterprising police officer cracked the case with … a Polish-English dictionary. *Prawo Jazdy* is Polish for "Driver's License." Ireland has many workers from Poland. When police officers pulled over a driver with a Polish driver's license, they mistook the words *Prawo Jazdy* for a Polish name and wrote the driver a ticket. The Polish drivers (all 50 of them) weren't about to correct the error.

Being monolingual — knowing only one language — can be a problem. It's also unusual. More people in the world are bilingual (speak two languages) or multilingual (speak three or more).

People whose mother tongue is English tend to be monolingual. Back in Shakespeare's time, English speakers spoke multiple languages. But now English is so universal that English speakers are less likely to bother learning other languages.

Some countries are language soups, with many languages adding their own flavors. India, for example, has a number of official languages. The national language is Hindi, but English is also used by government. Plus, each state has an official state language and usually recognizes other minority languages. In general, Indians are multilingual. For example, many people living in Kolkata, the capital of West Bengal, easily switch between Hindi, English and Bengali. They might also speak another two or three other languages depending on what they do or where they are from.

Even in India, though, where it's normal to speak many languages, some languages remain largely unknown. Only about 1000 people in a remote area of northeastern India speak Koro. Linguists stumbled upon it when they were researching another little-known language, Aka. Koro speakers live among Aka speakers, yet the two languages are as different as Japanese is from English. In a state with 120 languages, Koro speakers are gradually losing their language.

Koro, like 85 percent of languages in the world, is undocumented. This means it has not been written down or recorded — there are no dictionaries, books or sound recordings of it. Linguists from the Living Tongues Institute are racing to record some of the more endangered languages before they die out.

Another attempt to record languages is The Rosetta Project. It has samples of 1500 languages etched in tiny letters on a 7.5 cm (3 in.) diameter nickel disk. To read the tiny writing, you need a microscope to magnify the text 1000 times its size. The disk should last for thousands of years, and unlike computer discs that become useless when technology changes, it will be a permanent record of the languages.

IT'S ALL GREEK TO ME!

The Rosetta Project was inspired by the Rosetta Stone, a large stone from ancient Egypt carved with words.

The stone weighs about the same as three baby elephants (760 kg or 1675 lbs.) and dates back to March 27, 196 BCE. The same royal decree is inscribed on the stone three times: in hieroglyphs (the language of temple priests), demotic (the daily language of Egypt) and Greek (the administrative language). The Rosetta Stone allowed early linguists to decode Egyptian hieroglyphics for the first time by comparing the hieroglyphs on the stone to the Greek, a known language.

HOW LANGUAGES MORPH

AS AN ENGLISH SPEAKER, surely you recognize the opening three lines of *Beowulf*, the epic poem written in English about 1000 years ago?

> Hwæt. We Gardena in geardagum,
> þeodcyninga, þrym gefrunon,
> hu ða æþelingas ellen fremedon.

Okay, maybe you need some help. Here's the translation:

> Lo, praise of the prowess of people-kings
> of spear-armed Danes, in days long sped,
> we have heard, and what honor the athelings won!

The poem — all 3182 lines of it — is set in Scandinavia and tells the tale of Beowulf (the "bee hunter"), who battles with Grendel, Grendel's mother and a dragon. The poem was written in Old English, a form of English that looks like a foreign language to us.

All languages change over time. Reading the original *Canterbury Tales* — written in the 1300s — is easier than reading *Beowulf*, but you still have to work at it. Even Shakespeare's plays from the 1500s are written in a more formal style of English that forces you to think pretty hard. English has evolved rapidly in the last few centuries. But not all languages change so quickly — Japanese has stayed pretty much the same for 1000 years.

Over time, languages change in a few ways — through their vocabulary, word and sentence structure and pronunciation.

Vocabulary (words and their meanings) changes regularly. The words "knight" in English and *Knecht* in German have the same origin and meant "servant" or "slave." But the meaning of the English knight changed to someone with a high social rank who serves the king or queen. In German, though, a *Knecht* is still slaving away.

Sentence structure also changes. This happened to English when it collided with French during the Norman invasion in 1066. The Norman Conquest brought French rulers to the British Isles and changed English forever. The French introduced thousands of new words, such as "soup" and "salad." The French influence also led to a change in word order. Before French arrived, the word order in Old English was mostly SOV (Subject-Object-Verb). For example, in a translation from an Old English bible from the year 1000 you might find this: "Me ofthingth sothlice thaet ic hi worhte," which translates into: "Me displeases that I them made." After French took hold, the word order became what we know today, SVO (Subject-Verb-Object): "It displeases me that I made them."

Colliding languages can also change pronunciation. The arrival of French introduced (or reinforced) a new sound in English, the "zh" sound in the middle of the words "measure" and "pleasure."

Word pronunciation also changes because humans are energy savers. Some British people, for instance, say "f" instead of "th" because the "f" sound is easier and quicker to pronounce. So they'll say "Fursday" and "fink" instead of "Thursday" and "think." In a few generations, who knows — we English speakers may be singing "Happy Birfday"!

In North America, English speakers are big on yod-dropping — taking out the little "y" sound in some words. So "news" becomes "noos," "tune" becomes "toon," and "student" becomes "stoodent." (We don't drop the yod in all words, though. For example, "cute" and "fuse.") Dropping a sound is sometimes easier than pronouncing it.

THE GREAT VOWEL SHIFT

In the 1400s and 1500s, English speakers experienced a big change in pronunciation — suddenly how they said their vowels changed. Linguists call this the Great Vowel Shift. Before the Great Vowel Shift, the word "to" used to be pronounced "toe," "child" was pronounced "cheeld," and "loud" was "lewd." It's not known why the Great Vowel Shift occurred. The change marks the transition from Middle English to Modern English. Dutch and German had similar shifts.

Happy Birfday Felma

WHERE DO WORDS COME FROM?

IT'S 1539, AND A FIGHT breaks out between Spanish soldiers and the Native people of north-central Mississippi. To the Chickasaw people, the soldiers' metal armor and swords are new and dangerous. Their jingling and clanging is terrifying! A Native warrior who kills a soldier is given a special name, *asonnak-abi* (he who kills a person who jingles). *Asonnak-abi* became part of the language of the Chickasaw and, later, Choctaw people, but it changed in meaning over time. When Native warriors no longer fought soldiers wearing armor and wielding metal weapons, they began to use part of the word for other metal objects. *Asonnak* became the word for "kettle," "can," "bucket" and "cooking pan," passing from a war term to one of purely peaceful domestic use.

THAT SHAKESPEARE — WHAT A ZANY GUY

If you think the world is your oyster, thank William Shakespeare. The 16th century English writer invented, tweaked or made popular hundreds of phrases (such as "the world is my oyster") and words (such as "unearthly"). Shakespeare coined "fashionable," "puke" and "cheap." He liked to turn nouns into verbs. He "friended" long before Facebook. And we can thank him for "zany," too.

CHANGING CLIMATE, CHANGING WORDS

Even the climate can affect language. In Yup'ik, the language of the Yup'ik people of southwest Alaska, there are 70 words to describe what most of us would just call "ice." Global warming makes some of these words even more important than they once were. For example, *cikullaq* is newly formed ice. It's dangerous stuff for boaters. Historically, *cikullaq* occurred in October. Nowadays the word is used more frequently because *cikullaq* forms more often — ice now freezes and thaws many times over a winter as global temperatures rise.

Words: they come, they go, they change.

When a new idea or technology comes along, people change the way they talk to accommodate it — like the metal armor encountered by the Native people. In the last few decades, another technology has left its mark on language — computer technology. In fact, the word "computer" was originally used to refer to a person who did mathematical calculations, until the machines that did the same thing arrived.

New words, or neologisms, come about in other ways, too. Authors sometimes generate neologisms (*neo* means "new" and *log* means "word" in Greek). Jonathan Swift gave us "yahoo," a word he made up to describe a person without manners. J. K. Rowling gave us "muggle." And even the silly made-up words of Dr. Seuss have found their way into dictionaries. In 1950, he coined the word "nerd," which meant "a studious misfit." The meaning changed when it was applied to the computer industry. Creating better computers required studious, focused minds — people not easily distracted. Somehow, "nerd" morphed into a word for someone good with computers. Ironically, it was nerds who created Yahoo!, the successful Internet company. Jonathan Swift, meet Dr. Seuss!

Yahoo!

Nerd!

OUT WITH THE OLD . . .

A THOUSAND YEARS AGO, in *Beowulf*'s time, the idea of a "hero" was so important that Old English had lots of ways to describe one. *Beowulf*'s author used more than two dozen different words for hero. Today, even though there are lots of superheroes — Superman, Spiderman and so on — there's only one word for hero.

Languages constantly shed words when they are no longer needed. Every year, the *Oxford English Dictionary* (*OED*) retires words such as "mulomedic," "frutescent" and "vacivity." Hundreds of words are dropped every year. Ninety percent of written English uses only 7000 words, a tiny fraction of the words available, and little-used words are in danger of going the way of the dodo. This possibility so worried the people at the *OED* that they began the Adopt-a-Word program. Here's how it works. You choose a new word to adopt and use it every day. "Mulomedic" (medical care of a mule) might be hard to slide into a conversation. Try "frutescent." Although, "My, you look frutescent today" might not win you any friends. (It means "shrub-like," as in: "You look shrubby.") Or slip in "vacivity," which means "emptiness": "Without the word 'vacivity,' English speakers will feel a vacivity in their language."

My, you look frutescent today.

Old-fashioned words still have a place — in religious texts, poetry and in the legal profession. If it seems as if lawyers speak a different language from the rest of us, they do. Some of their words go back to medieval times, when lawyers used a combination of Latin, French and English. In an attempt to be super clear, they often paired words from different languages. "Breaking and entering," for example, came from a pairing of English and French words. "Will and testament" are from English and Latin.

Old vs. New

Match the old word with the more modern one of a similar meaning. (Answers on page 43.)

1. betwixt
2. durst
3. forsooth
4. hither
5. thither
6. mayhap
7. nary
8. nigh
9. prithee
10. swink
11. twain
12. fardel

a. burden
b. please
c. two
d. toil
e. dared
f. indeed
g. here
h. not any
i. there
j. near
k. between
l. possibly

LEGALESE

Legalese can be scarier than plain English. Take "subpoena," for example. A subpoena is a legal document informing someone that they must appear in court as a witness. It comes from the Latin words *sub poena* or "under penalty." Translation: "Failure to show up can land you in big trouble."

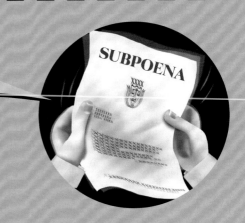

TALK LIKE A LAWYER

Confuse your friends and family by tossing around some lawyerly Latin.

in loco parentis (in place of a parent)
prima facie (a fact until proven otherwise)
nolo contendere (no contest)
res ipsa loquitur (the thing speaks for itself)
nemo dat quod non habet (no one gives what he has not)

... AND IN WITH THE NEW

"WOOT" IS A NEWCOMER to the English language. It originated in the 1990s and, in less than 20 years, made it into the *Oxford English Dictionary* (*OED*). Its etymology (origin) is unknown. "Netymologists" (people who use the Internet to track the origin of words and phrases) doggedly pursue woot's mysterious past, since it seems to have grown up with the Internet. It means "hurray!" as in: "I get to command the space station! Woot!"

Technology, as we've seen, is a big driver of neologisms (new words). Disasters, finance and food are also like solar power when it comes to words — the more energy that goes into them, the more new words that come out. Between 2000 and 2010, the online edition of the *OED* added about 100 000 new or revised words.

Here are some common ways to form new words:
- borrow or shorten (hippo for hippopotamus)
- back-form (grunge from grungy, or diplomat from diplomatic, or unit from unity)
- blend (stay + vacation = staycation)
- use acronyms (LOL = Laugh Out Loud)
- adapt people or place names (denim is from *serge de Nimes*, a fabric made in Nimes, France)

A new word can be created in an instant, but getting it into a dictionary takes time. The back-formed word "kidnap" was coined in the 1640s and 1650s. That's when British kids were taken by "kidnappers" — they were "napped" or "nabbed" (thief slang for "stolen") from their homes and sent to the colonies as servants. The public started to protest the practice, and by 1682, "kidnap" was in print. By 1729, it popped up in law dictionaries.

Today, lexicographers (people who compile dictionaries) wait for a new word to appear in print and online. They want to be sure that the word is here to stay. Before the digital age, it took about two or three years for lexicographers to even consider including a new word in a dictionary. The online world has sped up the process, especially with words that quickly gain fame — woot!

ROBERT CAWDREY'S TABLE ALPHABETICALL, PUBLISHED IN 1604, WAS THE FIRST ENGLISH DICTIONARY. IT CONTAINED 2543 WORDS (TODAY'S *OED* HAS 218 632) AND WAS WRITTEN "FOR THE BENEFIT OF LADIES, GENTLEWOMEN AND OTHER UNSKILLED FOLK."

SOFTWARE? GET OUT AND STAY OUT

Some countries have language police to keep their languages pure. For example, every year the French government replaces English words adopted into the language with newly created French words. At the turn of the last century, people used to say "software" because there was no French equivalent, until one was created — *logiciel*.

Want to bundernickle?

Definootly!

Create Your Own Words

You, too, can create a word by using one of the methods on page 30. Here are some words that people have recently invented. Can you figure out what they mean? (Answers on page 43.)

1. frenemy
2. freegan
3. hikikomori
4. steampunk
5. bargainous
6. babycino

How do you know when your new word is a success? If enough people use it for long enough, it's a word. Language is extremely democratic.

SLANGUISTICS

"YO HOMIE, YOU'RE looking thinkative. Whaddup?"

That's slang for: "Hey friend, you look deep in thought. What's going on?"

Slang is an informal word or phrase, usually found in speech, not writing. It is the poetry of everyday life. Slanguage can be regional or reflect a subculture, such as gamers, musicians or sports players. Slang is creative, contrary and slippery — here one moment, gone the next.

Some words are created for one occasion only. (Example: "This orange is juicilicious!") But others hang around long enough to make it into the dictionary.

The word "slang" itself was included in Noah Webster's *American Dictionary of the English Language* in 1828. Webster defined the word as "low, vulgar, unmeaning language" — in other words, nonstandard English looked down on by the educated. The largest group of slangarians (slang users) is people under the age of 25.

VICTORIAN SLANG

Back in Queen Victoria's day (the mid-1850s), a slangarian might say: "You're a fizzing fart catcher, aren't you? But I've seen you shake the elbow, and if you want me to shut my bone box and take your secret to the Earth bath, you'll have to pay me."

Translation: "You're a terrific valet, aren't you? But I've seen you gambling, and if you want me to keep my mouth shut and take your secret to the grave, you'll have to pay me."

SLANG, BIG BANG

Londoners who live in the east end of the city sometimes speak in Cockney rhyming slang. For example, Cockney for "girl" is the rhyming phrase "twist and twirl," which is usually shortened to just "twist." So girl = twist. There's little or no connection between the English word and its Cockney version, as you can see — Cockney is an insider language.

ENGLISH	RHYMES WITH	COCKNEY
feet	plates of meat	plates
teeth	Hampstead Heath	Hampsteads
legs	Scotch eggs	Scotches
eyes	mince pies	minces
arms	Chalk Farms	Chalk Farms
head	loaf of bread	loaf
mouth	north and south	north and south
face	boat race	boat race

loaf of bread

mince pies

boat race

plates of meat

Hampstead Heath

Scotch eggs

north and south

Chalk Farms

INVENTED LANGUAGES

qaStaH nuq?

nuqneH! THAT CAN BE roughly translated to "Hello!" But it really means: "What do you want?" in tlhIngan Hol, the language of the *Star Trek* warriors, the Klingons. In the 1980s, a linguist made up Klingon, as it's most often called, by creating a new vocabulary and grammar. More than 20 people speak Klingon fluently. That's more than the number who speak Ayapaneco, a Native language in Mexico. (As of 2013, Ayapaneco was spoken by only two elderly people.)

In the last 1000 years, hundreds of languages have been invented. One of the earliest to be written down was Lingua Ignota, which was created by a German nun named Hildegard von Bingen in the late 1100s. It has 23 letters and over 1000 words, mostly nouns that end in "z."

Constructed languages, or "conlangs," are either *a posteriori* or *a priori*. An *a posteriori* conlang is made up by altering the grammar and vocabulary of existing languages. *A priori* languages are constructed from scratch. Klingon is *a priori* and has the rarest word order — OVS (Object-Verb-Subject, see page 8). It also has sounds (but not words) that occur in a variety of languages. That's probably why Klingon sounds real and alien, besides the fact that Earthlings rarely say things like *"Dejpu'bogh Hov rur qabllj!"* ("Your face looks like a collapsed star!")

Conlangs often end up being insider languages — speak Klingon and you'll be a hit at a sci-fi convention, but no one else will understand you. While learning Klingon is good for you (as is learning any second language), it's mostly just for fun.

A few conlangs have more serious goals. An example is Blissymbolics, which was invented by Charles K. Bliss in 1949 to improve international communication. This conlang has around 100 basic symbols made of simple shapes that can be combined endlessly to form new meanings. The shape and position, plus other small indicators, give each symbol its sense. Since the 1970s, Blissymbolics has been taught to children with disabilities who have trouble communicating.

sky	earth	water	cloud	island
mouth	food	eye	cry	color
open	close	secret	sleep	box
person	mind	knowledge	give	teacher
happy	sad	upset	funny	home

But perhaps the best-known conlang is Esperanto, an *a posteriori* language. It was invented in 1887 by Ludwik Zamenhof, who believed that the world would be a better place if we all spoke a common language. Esperanto speakers sprang up all over the world, creating an international community, as Zamenhof had hoped. But the end result wasn't a better world. A group of disgruntled Esperantists broke away and invented Ido (translated as "offspring") in 1907. Neither language has replaced English as the lingua franca (common language for doing business) of the world.

Invent Your Own Language

For the movie *Avatar*, an anthropologist constructed Na'vi, a language spoken by the blue-skinned folk on planet Pandora. You can create your own language in four simple steps. (Okay, it's not simple, but it is fun.)

1. Decide on the sounds. (For example, maybe you decide that "ou" will always be pronounced "oo." So you would say: "Let's go oot and aboot.")
2. Write a vocabulary of words you use a lot.
3. Create grammar rules (see page 8 for some ideas on word order, for example).
4. Design a writing system.

KROKODILI — *TO CROCODILE, OR TO SPEAK IN YOUR NATIONAL LANGUAGE, AT AN EVENT WHERE YOU SHOULD BE SPEAKING ESPERANTO.*

WRITTEN LANGUAGE

THE AMAZING THING ABOUT putting thoughts in writing is that your words can last beyond your lifetime. We still read books that were written long ago. Their authors are long dead, but not their words.

Writing is a set of symbols that represent the sounds of a language. As with spoken language, it's impossible to pin down the origin of writing. But let's zoom back 35 000 years to look for clues in the caves of long-ago France. The cave walls are alive with animals. In among paintings of mammoths, horses and rhinos are lines, zigzags and semicircles. Doodles? Nope. A closer look by archaeologists revealed a pattern of close to 30 symbols that pop up in various caves in Europe. Straight lines and dots are the most common, but there are also squares, circles and triangles. The symbols may have been a form of prewriting that originated in Africa and was brought to Europe by the early humans who migrated there.

CHANCES ARE YOUR ANCESTORS WERE ILLITERATE. IN THE MID-1800s, ONLY ABOUT 10 PERCENT OF THE ADULTS IN THE WORLD COULD READ OR WRITE. TODAY, IT'S MORE THAN 80 PERCENT.

In ancient Iraq, the Sumerians developed a writing system by about 3200 BCE. Early symbols that represented animals or objects eventually evolved into cuneiform — wedge-shaped symbols made by pressing a pointed reed into a moist clay tablet.

Cuneiform lasted about 3000 years and was used to record business transactions related to property, inventory and taxes. It was also used to track other important information such as daily beer rations (allowances) for workers. The Sumerians found new uses for cuneiform beyond bookkeeping. They used it for historical records, letters and literature. Close to Sumeria, and even earlier, the Egyptians also created a writing system.

Like the Sumerians and Egyptians, other cultures in ancient India, China, Mexico and Greece invented their own writing systems. In most of these cultures, only scribes or priests could write. At the palace of Nestor, at Pylos in ancient Greece, only 35 or so scribes wrote 1000 clay tablets in just a few months. Eventually, more people (mostly men) were educated and learned how to write, but it took thousands of years for writing to filter down to the masses. Writing was powerful stuff, and the most powerful people wanted to keep it for themselves.

WHICH WAY?

Egyptian hieroglyphs could be written in any direction. The people and animals pictured in the hieroglyphs always face the beginning of a line, showing readers which direction to read.

THE ART OF WRITING

Like art, writing probably developed at different times and in different places. Evidence of ancient writing keeps turning up unexpectedly. Sixty-thousand-year-old ostrich eggshells etched with the same symbols over and over were found in a rock shelter in South Africa. The 270 shell fragments span 5000 years. What did the marks mean? No one knows. Maybe "Hands off, this is Zeb's egg."

WHICH ALPHABET?

WHEN YOU WERE LEARNING how to read, you probably pointed to a word with your finger and sounded out the l-e-t-t-e-r-s. You likely pronounced "knife" with the "k" sound and puzzled over why the words "gnu," "knew" and "new" all sounded the same. It would make sense for an alphabet to have one symbol represent one sound. Some do, but some don't.

The Finns have it easy. Their writing system is one of the most phonetic in the world — one letter represents one sound. Finnish children learning to read just sound out the letters. English is a mix of phonetics and some things you just have to learn, such as not pronouncing the "k" in "knife" or the "g" in "gnu." Chinese has mostly visual symbols that may or may not indicate pronunciation.

WHAT A CHARACTER!

Chinese script was invented about 5000 years ago and, after some changes, has remained the same for the past 2000 years. Many Chinese characters in ancient texts can still be recognized by today's Chinese readers.

The Chinese word *zhōng* means "middle." It's represented by a line through the middle of a box, which represents an enclosure:

UP, DOWN, LEFT, RIGHT

你肯定是想要一面
美观的国旗吧，当这样的
都上空迎风飘扬（让我们
都），或当你的军队高举
昂首行进（假设你也有一
情景真教人热泪盈眶呢。

Many writing systems switch writing direction if needed. Chinese is traditionally written vertically. Yet in the last century, it has more often been written horizontally, left to right, as shown here. The switch might be related to the speed of reading. Our field of vision is wider horizontally than vertically. In tests, skilled readers of Chinese read horizontal text faster than vertical text: 580 characters a minute horizontally compared with 260 characters a minute vertically.

No writing system is better than another, just different. Finnish script has efficiency, Chinese script has variety, and English writing has a bit of both.

Phonetic alphabets evolved from the alphabets of the Semitic languages of the Middle East about 3500 years ago. The people there developed alphabets that had consonants (b, c, d, f and so on) but no vowels (a, e, i, o, u and sometimes y). *Whvr ws rdng wld fll n th vwl snds!*

Hebrew and Arabic, two Semitic languages, added vowel sounds by making marks above and below the letters. For example, the Hebrew word for "camel" is spelled *Gimel* (ג), *Mem* (מ), *Lamed* (ל). Written right to left, as Hebrew is, it becomes: גָּמָל. It is pronounced "gum mall." (The stress is on "mall.") The little "Ts" under the symbols represent the vowel sounds. They are called *nikud* and are mostly used for young readers and those new to the language.

Semitic alphabets eventually led to phonetic alphabets, such as ancient Greek. At first, the ancient Greeks wrote in any direction. Even in a spiral. Aswritingevolveditcametobewrittenlefttorightandgradually spaces were introduced between words, and then punctuation was added. Without punctuation, "Let's eat Grandma!" means something different from "Let's eat, Grandma!" Thank you, Greeks.

Other writing systems assign symbols to syllables instead of letters. Syllables are usually a vowel sound with a consonant on either side. For example, "monkey" has two syllables — "mon" and "key." The North American Native languages Cree, Inuktitut and Cherokee use syllabic scripts created for their written languages. Cherokee was the first Native North American language to be written down in its own unique writing system. In 1819, a Cherokee named Sequoyah noticed that marks on paper were used to represent English, so he invented a writing system for his own language using 85 symbols. In Cherokee, "buffalo" is *ya na sa*, or in Cherokee script: ꮹꮎꮜ

ꮹ = *ya*   ꮎ = *na*   ꮜ = *sa*

UNSPOKEN LANGUAGES

IN THE 1500s, THE EMPEROR of Hindustan, Akbar the Great, had an idea he wanted to test — would babies raised without spoken language learn to speak? And if they did, what language would they speak? Maybe, he thought, they would speak the original language first spoken by humans. If so, what a discovery!

Although the experiment is real, the details are fuzzy. Anywhere from 12 to 30 babies were raised in a house with mute nurses. When they were about four years old, Akbar visited them. He heard not a sound. The children gestured to communicate. Either they had created their own sign language, or they had learned to sign from their nurses. Akbar considered the experiment a failure because the babies didn't speak. But linguists say he missed the point — maybe the first human language was sign language.

Humans come up with ways to communicate whether they can hear or not. A language you can speak with your hands is an obvious solution, and there are many examples of sign languages throughout history. In fact, the world's newest language is a sign language. It's a community-based language called Al Sayyid Bedouin and is spoken in a village of 3500 people in the Negev Desert, Israel. About 150 members of the community are deaf, but everyone signs.

BABY BABBLE

Babies, deaf or hearing, babble between six and ten months old. Hearing babies make "nonsense" sounds from their mother tongue, as well as other "foreign" sounds. Deaf babies do the same, but they do it with hand gestures. Babbling — with sounds or gestures — is how babies learn to communicate.

Most sign languages have specific hand movements for different words. In British Sign Language, a signer needs two hands to spell. In American Sign Language (ASL), only one hand is needed.

But sometimes there is no sign for a word, and it has to be spelled out letter by letter. Below is the ASL finger spelling alphabet. Try finger spelling your name and where you were born.

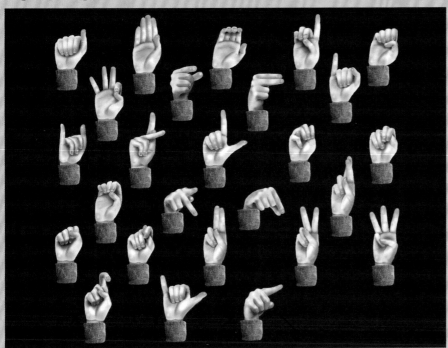

Today, there are schools all over the world to teach sign language to the deaf. The first one was inspired by the deaf community in the Paris slums of the 1700s. The community had created a sign language, and in 1771, a priest named Charles-Michel de l'Épée decided to set up a school to teach it. Épée changed the sign language that was already in use and in doing so made it clumsy. Still, this early French sign language was later brought to a school for the deaf in the United States.

What happened next happens to languages everywhere. The sign language changed and got more complex. American Sign Language evolved mostly from the French and other American sign languages, including a sign language used on Martha's Vineyard. (The early settlers of Martha's Vineyard, an island off the coast of Massachusetts, had a high proportion of deaf people, who passed on deafness through their genes. A local sign language evolved as the deaf community grew.)

Other countries developed their own sign languages, which are completely different from ASL. For example, in ASL to sign the verb "cook" you quickly clap your hands together twice, then flip over the top hand and hit it against the palm of the lower hand. The same sign in Danish means "interpret." In Chinese Sign Language, the sign for "father" is the sign for "secret" in ASL.

Sign languages are different from one another — and from the dominant spoken languages of the area. ASL users who also speak English are bilingual, since ASL is as different from English as it is from Danish Sign Language.

THE LAST WORD

WHEN YOU WERE STILL IN diapers, you learned to speak. By age three, you were talking in complete sentences and chitchatting away to everyone around you. Just like meowing comes naturally to a cat, and barking to a dog, language comes naturally to you.

Language, however, allows you to communicate, and it allows others, alive and dead, to communicate with you. Through language you learn about great ideas, the natural world and other people.

Languages are what make us human, and we need to preserve as many of them as possible. Why? As an old Czech proverb says: *"Kolik řečí znáš, tolikrát jsi člověkem."* The literal translation in English is: "The number of languages you know, that many times you are a person [human being]." In other words, the more languages you speak, the richer your life.

So now that you've mastered one language, why not try learning another one? It's an easy step from "Hello, how are you?" to *"Hola, ¿cómo estás?"* in Spanish, or *"Bonjour, comment ça va?"* in French, or *"Konnichiwa, ogenki desu ka?"* in Japanese, or *"Jak se máš?"* in Czech.

Good luck! Or, to translate that into Bengali, *"Shubheccha roilo!"*

ANSWERS

SOUND SYMBOLS (page 11)

1 a, 2 a, 3 b, 4 a, 5 b, 6 b, 7 a, 8 b, 9 a, 10 a

LANGUAGE FAMILIES (page 14)

1. *bonus, melior, optimus*: good, better, best
2. *incredibilis*: incredible, unbelievable
3. *fortunatus*: fortunate, lucky, happy
4. *benevolentia*: benevolence, kindness, good will
5. *perfectus*: complete, finished, done/perfect, without flaw
6. *excellentia*: excellence, merit, worth

OLD vs. NEW (page 29)

1 k, 2 e, 3 f, 4 g, 5 i, 6 l, 7 h, 8 j, 9 b, 10 d, 11 c, 12 a

CREATE YOUR OWN WORDS (page 31)

1. An enemy disguised as a friend
2. A person who eats food that's been discarded
3. Someone who avoids social contact
4. Science fiction that takes place during the steam era, about 200 years ago
5. Less than the usual cost — a great bargain
6. Frothed, warm milk

GLOSSARY

bilingual: able to speak two languages

culture: a group of people who have things in common, such as beliefs, language, religion, food and music

cuneiform: one of the earliest forms of writing, developed about 5200 years ago in the Middle East

DNA: Deoxyribose Nucleic Acid, a substance in living cells that contains the instructions — scientists call them genes — for all living things

endangered: in danger of becoming extinct

etymology: the study of word origins

extinct: no longer existing

genes: the instructions in DNA passed from living things to their offspring

grammar: the rules of a language

hieroglyphics: an ancient Egyptian writing system

illiterate: unable to read or write

language family: a group of languages that share a common ancestor language

lexicographers: the people who create dictionaries

lingua franca: the common language for doing business among people of diverse languages

linguists: the people who study languages

monolingual: able to speak only one language

multilingual: able to speak three or more languages

neologisms: new words

phonetic: the sounds of speech

Romance languages: languages descended from the Latin spoken by the Romans

slang: informal words, more commonly spoken than written

syntax: how words are arranged to form sentences

INDEX